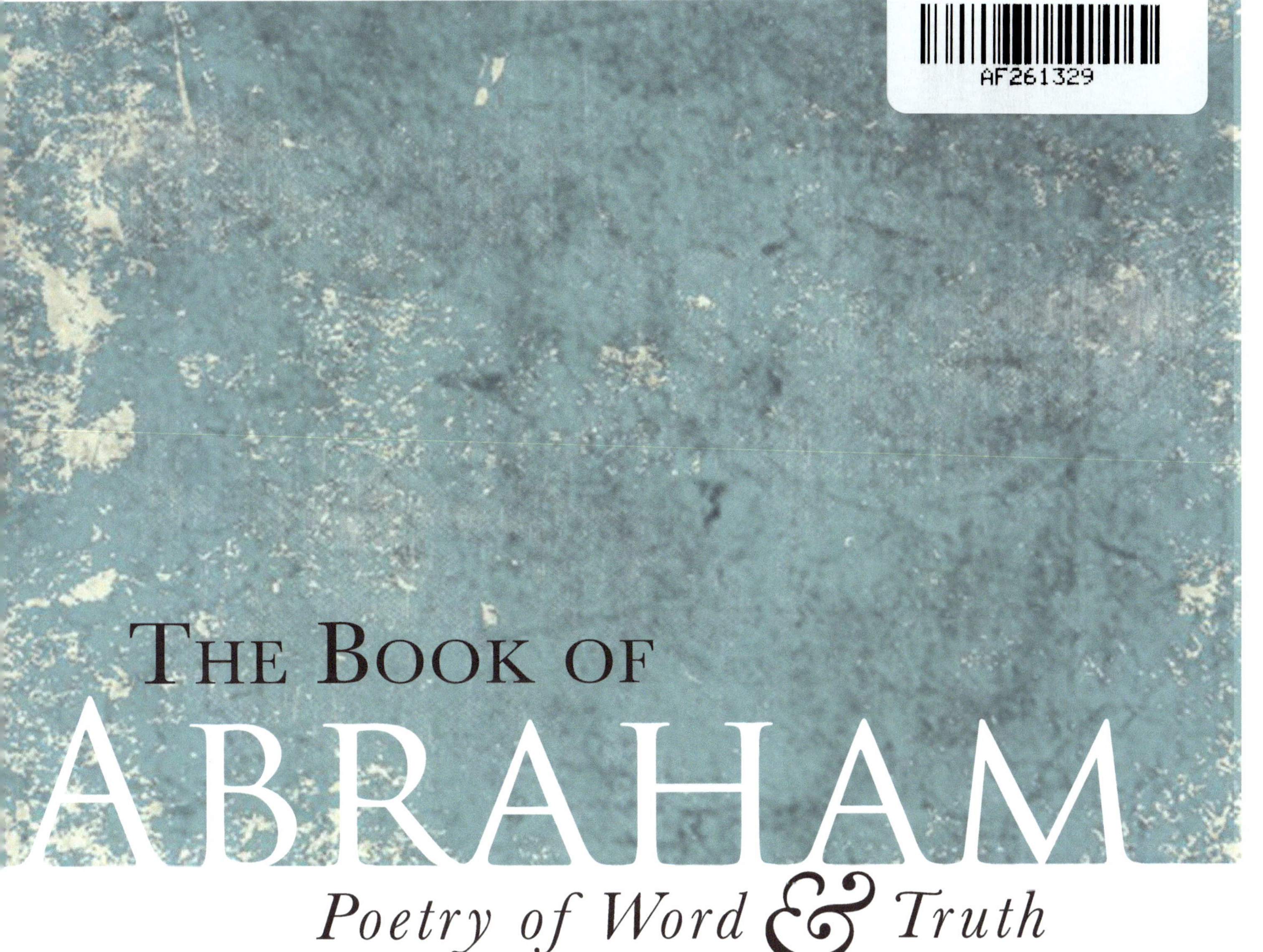

THE BOOK OF
ABRAHAM

Poetry of Word & Truth

ISBN 978-1-5136-3886-7
Produced by www.pamricedesign.com
Design/Layout: www.pamricedesign.com
Book illustrated by Pamela C. Rice
First Edition Printing 2018

The Book of ABRAHAM

Poetry of Word & Truth

ILLUSTRATED BY PAMELA C. RICE

Table of Contents

ABOUT THE AUTHOR

Mr. Bolden was born to Daniel and Ophelia Bolden in East St. Louis, Illinois on January 19, 1935. He attended Lincoln High School and, upon graduation, entered Lincoln University in Jefferson City, Missouri. Mr. Bolden graduated cum laude from Lincoln University with a B.A. in music composition.

Later, Abraham Bolden married his long time friend and schoolmate, Barbara L. Hardy, to whom he was married for 49 years prior to her death. To that marriage were born 3 children, Ahvia Maria, Abraham Jr., and Dr. Daaim Shabazz. He also has two grandchildren, Ismail and Cydni.

After graduating from Lincoln University, Mr. Bolden became the first African American Detective to be employed by the Pinkerton National Detective Agency. After leaving the detective agency, he served as a State Highway Patrolman in the State of Illinois. Continuing to advance in the field of police work, he became a member of the United

States Secret Service in October of 1960. Mr. Bolden met
President John F. Kennedy in Chicago, Illinois and, after
a brief conversation with Bolden, President Kennedy was
instrumental in making Mr. Bolden the first African-American
to be assigned to the Secret Service White House Detail
in Washington, D.C.

Mr. Bolden served in the U.S. Secret Service from 1960
to 1964. He lives in Chicago and is retired after working for
thirty years in the field of quality-control supervision. Since
the release of his book, Mr. Bolden has been requested for
a variety of radio, TV, and newspaper interviews, as well as
speaking engagements.

*ABRAHAM BOLDEN is the author of **The Echo from Dealey
Plaza**: The true story of the first African American on the
White House Secret Service detail and his quest for justice
after the assassination of JFK.*

ABOUT THE ARTIST

Pamela C. Rice, always an artist, has had many one-woman shows and has exhibited in galleries in the tristate area. Three 'table-top' volumes of her paintings have been published. For the past three years Rice has been instructing *Pam Rice's Painting Workshops*, a method that trains beginning artists how to paint in one session.

Rice grew up surrounded by creative art and design, and believes that she is a person born to write and illustrate for children. Both Pam's father and brother were in the field of graphic design. Her father, a commercial artist, and her brother was in textile and artesian design.

With over 30 years of independent and corporate experience in advertising, graphic design, and visual communications, Rice has earned high recognition and top accolades with over 40 design awards. She has made guest appearances as a lecturer at the Illinois Academy of Design and Merchandising and at Northeastern Illinois University. She has also taught at Alverno College and the University of Illinois-Chicago, Principal Scholar's Program.

Creating children's books is what Pamela C. Rice enjoys and since August 2015 she has released fifteen books. Each book is warmly illustrated by Rice and offers written artistic expression of her childhood experiences. They are inspirations that children will find fun, imaginative and educational. She is currently working to bring more diversity and inclusion to her library of books.

"Mr. Bolden's *The Book of Abraham — Poetry of Word &* *Truth* gave me an opportunity to explore a different and editorial illustrative technique in interpreting his prose."

Forward

By, Andrew Mount

These poems and writings of Truth are authored by the first African-American Secret Service Agent to work the White House Detail. The President engaged Bolden in a conversation in which the President invited Bolden to become the first African American to be appointed to the Secret Service White House Detail in April of 1961.

After serving on the White House Secret Service Detail, and observing conduct and attitudes of some of the detail agents that tended to place the president's life in jeopardy Bolden reported his concerns to the then Chief of the United States Secret Service. After the president was assassinated as predicted by Bolden, Bolden was subsequently brought up on false charges of bribery, convicted and sentenced to six years in prison.

What is past is prologue, said the Bard.

Bolden's life today centers around the solution to humanity's enduring problems. It is important for readers to know that Bolden is a teacher of spiritual empowerment and capable of shedding light upon the function of consciousness in humankind. "We are all One," says the former paladin of official justice who risked his own freedom to stand for truth. "We have to learn how to do things that correlate with each other, to develop our spiritual capacities, to become unified in thought, word and deed. Suffering is the greatest teacher, yet there is advantage in the spiritual world because we are purified to do a greater work."

Bolden's writings are intended to spark a revolution in consciousness and liberate humanity from age-old falsehoods and beliefs. Bolden believes that we as a people (worldwide) must move toward the plane of the Higher Self, and use the suffering of past and present day occurrences as a platform to rise to the plane of the Spiritual Self, the God within. These are the indispensable components of Bolden's Spiritual, Mental, and Physical philosophies. May the Infinite Hierarchies of our Lord guide him in his endeavor.

YOUTH

Can we hear the ominous thunder rolling?

A new day is by God's Will unfolding.

Our youth are being subconsciously guided,

To a land where Mankind is one, undivided.

The lion and sheep lay side by side,

Tis a land where Love and Truth abide.

Stone brick and mortar has left them in a lurch

In young pure flesh, God is building His church.

Inside the Divine Mind Holy Angels shall sing,

A new song from Heaven to Earth they shall bring.

Trading guns and wars for wisdom and reason,

Their hearts shall bear sweet fruit in every season.

God is working within them to still hate's voices,

Giving Justice and Equity the favorite of choices.

Let elders and seniors be not dismayed,

We fought a good fight, our debts have been paid.

The youth that you see shall walk in God's light

To bring about day and vanquish the darkness of night.

ABRAHAM W. BOLDEN

THE OLE MAN

The ole man in the window

Sits looking through the glass,

How quickly has the years gone by,

So swiftly time did pass.

Once only concerned

With loss and gain,

His worries now are

Aches and pain,

Children gone…

He sits alone

Peering into the distance

Through the window pane

Revisiting life's joys and sorrows

Waiting for destinies'

Uncertain tomorrows

As the years sped by,

Memories that make the

Ole man laugh or cry….

(Continued)

THE OLE MAN *(Continued)*

Bouncing babies on his knee,
Throwing them into the air
And hollowing "wheeee"
Coming home from work
On a sunlit day,,
Watching shining faces
Scamper about in play…
Gazing……, blankly staring….,
Remembering the wedding day
When two hearts said "I do"……..
Love you…I do love you…..
The ole man in the window
Sits looking through the glass,
How quickly has the years gone by,
So swiftly time did pass.

ASCENSION

Unless one's mind
In GNOSIS abide,
All that can be seen
Is God's Backside.
The mortal Soul that
Awakens to
LOVE through GRACE
Must die whilst alive
To see God's face.

The Initiation

Making my way through the
Pathway of life,
I was fleeing from a sordid
World filled with bigotry and strife.
I came upon a little wooden house
Surrounded by tall and stately
Elm wood trees
Their branches bowing and bending
In the cool summer breeze.
I approached the solitary structure
It's outside was unpainted,
Walked up the three steps,
As if I was acquainted,
Had knocked upon this door,
In ancient times before.
This room with the three legged table,
Resting upon a bare wooden floor.

(Continued)

THE INITIATION *(Continued)*

An elderly distinguished man

His hair as white as snow,

Dressed in a robe bearing many symbols,

That only God's Sages know.

Laying upon a table

Between flail and crook

In the single candlelight

There suddenly appeared to sight,

Words of a primeval book,

Describing the ascent of Nations

To a peak of excellence

Their enmity toward Love Divine….

Their fall into decadence.

"There is no multitude,

All creation is One,

Born of the Mother Nature

And the energizing Father Sun.

For this cause did I come,

THE INITIATION

In the manifest to see,
The marvels of my creation
When in the beginning, I said "Be".
"And when eyes close
In nature's sacred place,
Once again I shall meet you
Face to face."
"Repeat after me,"
The bearded teacher said…
My soul became enlivened,
My body seemed as dead.
"My life is for God,
No assistant has He,
There was nothing in existence,
All Spirits are contained within
And are one Holy Consistency,
All that is, is ME,"
"Place your daunting fear aside

(Continued)

THE INITIATION   *(Continued)*

I will be your voice

For to abide in darkness

Or the light of wisdom

Is Man's free will and choice.

To the unbeliever,

Let your ears become deaf,

Call upon all creatures to

'Know thyself'.

Awakened from my blessed sleep,

I vowed to God my oath to keep,

And that as I write these sincere words today,

Others will be initiated

Along life's way.

BALANCE

A "Negro" has no enforceable rights that this country must respect,

That's what a Supreme Court Justice ruled and the populace didn't object.

For over 400 years laws have come and promises dead and gone,

When will America correct and erase this prevailing egregious wrong?

Far away from Africa, shackled on a ship, considered as property and slave,

Now fighting in wars against America's enemies, no man has been
more brave.

In the mountains of Afghanistan and in the heat of the desert's sand,

He has given up the ultimate sacrifice while treated as three fifths of a man.

She nursed the "Missa's" crying babies and picked the "Massa's" cotton;

His flesh rotted on the end of the whip, her humanity long forgotten.

Woe be to the dictum that disenfranchised the human rights of man,

For surely God's balance wheel shall turn and the low shall be high again.

WE MARCH FOR JOBS
WE DEMAND VOTING RIGHTS NOW!
WE DEMAND AN LA NO
UAW SAYS END SEGREGATED RULES IN PUBLIC SCHOOLS
JOBS FOR ALL NOW!
WE DEMAND EQUAL RIGHTS NOW!
MARCH
P.RCE

A Good Man

Oh Lord of Light
And darkness too
I kneel down asking
What can good men do?
We've marched and sang,
The songs of Peace,
But yet our souls find no release.
Our patience is fragile,
Wickedness is liberally sown;
How can man now
Be spiritually reborn?
The voice of rolling thunder
Answered passionately.
"Find the straight path
There I will be;
And behold a wonder
A hot blazing fire
In it crucify your lower self
The "weak-isms" of bodily desire.'"
Throw hate into the cleansing sea;
Hear the sweet refrains of love's melody;
Merge your heart with all creations that be.
"Love your neighbor as I love you;
Those are the prayers that good men do."

REFLECTIONS

Let all the elders of our blessed nation take note;
Our children are acting out the horrid script that
WE wrote;
Banning of guns is not an effective answer
So long as our hearts are filled with the cancer,
Of evil thoughts and subtle malicious deeds
That robs our fellow travelers of the precious needs
To find peace in our minds and love in our hearts
And the Faith and brotherhood that never departs.
What we see in the mirror that truly reflects,
The seeds we have planted sprouting bitter regrets
And violence and murders while school bells ring,
While religions look overhead for a coming King;
But chaos will reign and death's angel shall ride,
Until WE banish the hate and let God's love abide.

Happiness
RAGE
GREED
SELFISHNESS

Nature's balance

Just as water is the adversary of a flaming fire,

Happiness is subdued by unwarranted desire.

Barren soil makes little use of the revitalizing rain,

Greed is never satisfied by ruthless and selfish gain.

The peak of a mountain holds the sparkling snow,

That provides the fresh water to life in the valley below.

The high feeds the low and the low feeds the high;

All needs are furnished by the earth and the sky.

So give of your love to your fellow man

For what one cannot do, many willing souls can.

Lust, rage and greed, the gates to hell, avoid;

And in all of your strivings, remember your Lord.

Woe, Woe, Woe

"Woe , Woe , Woe,"
The frightened people said
They have shot our dashing leader
In the front of his forehead;
Arriving on a mission
Of a brotherhood journey;
He lays now naked
On a bloody hospital gurney.
Agents stood watching
From near and afar,
Some had spent the night
In a strip club bar,
Blood shot eyes
Showed the color red,
Agents stood with fixed feet
As they shot our leader dead
Assassins followed him closely

(Continued)

WOE, WOE, WOE   *(Continued)*

From state to state,
With rifles at the ready
And hearts full of hate.
"We'll murder him for sure,"
A crazed conspirator vowed
They mingled and hide themselves
In the Dallas, Texas crowd.
Bang! Bang! went the sound
Of guns at noon that sunnyl day
Motors roaring and cars speeding
Along the Stemmons Freeway,
A hero, a father, a man of empathy,
A thinker, Christian
A man of bravery.
A casket borne down
Pennsylvania Avenue,
Carrying a man that envisioned

A B R A H A M   W .   B O L D E N

Woe, Woe, Woe

Justice for me and for you.

He wanted Peace and Harmony

And a level playing field

For all Americans, Black or, White

Was his sincere appeal

"Woe , Woe , Woe,"

The frightened people said

They have shot our dashing leader

In the front of his head;

Arriving on a mission

Of a peacemaking journey;

He lays now dead

On a bloody hospital gurney.

BITTER FRUIT

Falling from a wicked tree;

Whose roots sprout from selfish hearts

Where "I" is more valued than "we".

Watered by the rain

That fertilizes the pain

Of the young and unborn

Proliferating thickets and thorns

That we weaved into crowns

Separating white from the brown.

Immersed in wretched greed

To satisfy an imagined need…..

The need to dominate

With minds that are reprobate.

We have drank from the chalice

Of hate, murder and malice

Asking our children

To march in a pilgrim

(Continued)

BITTER FRUIT *(Continued)*

To peace and understanding
While we are demanding…….
Demanding that they pursue
Our perverted teaching
And our hypocritical preaching
Of truth, love and harmony
While we water that wicked tree
Thinking that from the Almighty
We are hidden…
Working deeds that are forbidden.
We have created a drunken society
Rejecting God's Divine sobriety.
Yea, young men and women,
Disturb the sea!
Change the order,
Of things that be!
Sing a new song

Bitter Fruit

Be steadfast and strong;
For, know that it's true
That Our God is with you.
And YOU finally shall prevail
Over man's created hell.
In Love's bosom shall you dwell
MARCH ON! MARCH ON!
The Holy Essence be with you.

BENIGHTED

Hung and dismembered in the tall oak trees;
The rancid stench of a cruel act polluted the
Hot sticky breeze.
A people benighted by the power
Of God,
Their backs now scarred by the
Whip and the rod.
A people existing since
The dawn of creation,
Their Black skins now symbols
Of a once golden nation.
Natufians, Moors, Alkebulans,
The ancients from Mu,
Scientist, Chemist and Doctors too,
Astrologers, Ship builders,
Healers of the blind,
Forced to endure indignities
Of every evil kind.

(Continued)

BENIGHTED   *(Continued)*

Explorers of the Ama-Ra-Ka
Thousands of years ago,
Now considered as beasts,
Because false history
Made it so.
Mastering the trade winds
Of North, West, and South
They navigated every river,
From dry land to ocean's mouth.
Known as the Deng, Su and the Khemite
Took civilization to every land,
Mutilated bodies swinging back and forth
Considered, now, three fifths of a man.
Hung and dismembered in the tall oak trees;
The rancid stench of a cruel act polluted the
Hot sticky breeze.
A people benighted by the power
Of God,
Their backs now scarred by the
Whip and the rod.

ABRAHAM W. BOLDEN

THE CAPTIVE

THE CAPTIVE *(Continued)*

They stomped their heels against his face,

And filled his bloody nose with the stench of mace,

His coat of many colors laid soiled on the ground,

His once strong body, their deceptions had bound.

They pushed him toward the pitch-black cave,

With intent that this would become his grave.

Women fainted at the sight and screamed aloud,

But they continued to trample him,

They were the arrogant and the proud.

He had come from God to bring the Light,

To turn man's heart from wretches to right.

They pierced his feet and shackled his hands,

They made a noose of hardened black iron bands,

They labeled him a beast below human man

And ground his face in the hot desert sand.

"Kill him, Kill him!" The rabble cried,

"To overthrow our ruler-ship, this daemon has tried".

"He's nothing but a thief and outcast knave,

"He claims the whole world only God can save".

THE CAPTIVE

A shining sword pierced his trembling thigh,

As beams of Heavenly Light shone in the sky.

The rolling thunders spoke deeply and said,

"None but GOD heals your sick and raises your dead".

"Loose Him, Loose him! Set him free,

Or a burning hell, I will make for thee".

The rabble stopped suddenly and bent their knees,

The hurricanes of suffering became

Like a summer breeze.

"My words have been with him throughout

Aeon's youth.

He's the Anointed Savior of Mankind,

His name is DIVINE TRUTH."

P.RICE

THE WEB

You spiders have ruled this temporal world,
The leader of the insects said;
You've killed and murdered all your days,
And caused billions of us to lay dead.
The Spiders looked surprised at them,
Who once were mighty foes;
But now they lingered in the Spider's nest,
Decrying their many woes.
You promised us freedom and justice too,
You are a monstrous liar;
You tricked us here from the land of Mu,
From the fertile land to this briar.
The Spider licked his slippery lips,
And looked up toward the sky;
Amazed at the truthful and fearless words,
Being spoken by the fly.
What can we do? The Spider asked,

(Continued)

THE WEB *(Continued)*

What is your heartfelt demand?

"To become like you and in riches bask,

On the beaches and shores of sand!"

The Spider turned away his face,

To hide his sinister grin.

I anoint you as leader in this place,

And death's eternal friend.

THE ARMOUR

We wrestle not with flesh and blood; but with principalities and powers of darkness. They have cut off the souls of MAN at the cross beam that separates man from the beasts of the field. To be regenerated, MAN must submit to Divine reflection and destroy the beast within through repentance, submission to the higher SELF, TRUST IN GOD, abstinence, meditation, sincerity, and most of all, "do unto others as you would have others do unto you." This leads to LOVE, the cure for all societal ailments.

Garbage In...

Garbage in, Garbage out;

Is what this ephemeral world is all about

What ever happened to "Yes we can"

'Twas just another dream of disillusioned Man.

A nation preaching love and hope,

While hanging foreign leaders on the end of a rope;

Round green button near a big fat thumb,

Ready to release destruction with a megaton bomb.

Garbage in, Garbage out;

Is what this ephemeral world is all about

What ever happened to "Yes we can"

'Twas just another dream of disillusioned Man.

Babbling sacred scripture and God we quote,

While separating head from body at the throat;

Smell of stinking death filling earth's blessed air,

Believing that victory makes monstrous deeds fair.

Garbage in, Garbage out;

(Continued)

GARBAGE IN... *(Continued)*

Is what this ephemeral world is all about

What ever happened to "Yes we can"

'Twas just another dream of disillusioned Man.

Dead bodies growing like a field of wheat,

Elected leaders murdered in the middle of the street;

Sweet words of peace written by a hired grammarian,

To conceal the inner motives of a true barbarian;

Garbage in, Garbage out;

Is what this ephemeral world is all about

What ever happened to "Yes we can"

'Twas just another dream of disillusioned Man.

SOUL

My Soul longs to hear
That once familiar sound,
Of Heaven's workmen tilling
God's fertile garden ground
Birds chirping in the trees,
Wings searching for the springlike breeze
That will bear them afloat.
Feathers adorned like a multicolored coat
Singing melodious music of love Divine
To nations of every race and kind.
The Wars and bigotry,
Forever defeated
The errors of mankind
Go unrepeated.
Men digging and sowing
The seeds of Knowing,
That he, his God,

(Continued)

SOUL *(Continued)*

And his fellow man

Are one creation since

This mortal existence began.

Come brother, Come sister

In Peace, let us dwell,

Let us live in Fellowship'

And seal the rustic gates

That leads to a discordant hell.

My Soul longs to hear

That once familiar sound,

Of Heaven's workmen tilling

God's fertile garden ground

THE MIRROR

Oh how God's mirror hanging on the wall
Foretells the reality of Man's ignominious fall
Revealing Truths that our minds recall
Reflecting our deeds both great and small.
They are masterfully made and full of life
Showing us the good times and those of strife.
The images hate what we hate,
And love what we love.
Those little spotless mirrors,
Sent from the mystic world of creation above.
These sacred mirrors born so pure and clean
Prepared by Holy hands in a Temple unseen,
Not a crack or a defect in the smooth glossy surface,
Not a defect or blemish to warrant its replace
In front of the mirror stood a man with a gun,
An automatic rifle bought for having fun;
But for violence and murder used to conquer the land,

(Continued)

The Mirror   *(Continued)*

Showing no mercy for anyone be they woman or man

He sowed his vibrations in young mirrors to come

Unwary that he in the mirror would follow

The beat of his drum

"What's happening, what's happening?" the societies shout,

"What are these horrendous killings all about?"

It's the man in the mirror that lost his way,

The debts of his fathers

The young must pay.

ISBN: 978-1-5136-3886-7

PRINTED IN U.S.A.